J
523.5
Bra   Branley, Franklyn M.
       Shooting stars.

12.95

JE 19 '96	DATE DUE	
JE 29 '96		OCT 0 1 2012
JY 3 '96		JUL 3 1 2013
JY 10 '96	MAY 0 8 2010	DEC 2 1 2015
JUL. 25 1996	JAN 3 2001	MAY 0 4 2017
AUG. 20 1996	JUL 2 1 2001	JUL 1 1 2017
OCT. 2 1996	JUL 2 4 2001	JUL 1 5 2019
FEB. 4 1999	APR 0 7 2004	APR 1 6 2021
FEB. 27 1999	JAN 2 9 2008	
OCT. 27 1999	NOV 2 9 2008	
MAR. 1 6 2000	Aug 19 2009	
APR. 03 2000	9-17-10	

Shooting Stars

by Franklyn M. Branley   illustrated by Holly Keller

Thomas Y. Crowell   New York

Other Recent Let's-Read-and-Find-Out Science Books® You Will Enjoy

A Drop of Blood • My Five Senses • What Happened to the Dinosaurs? • Switch On, Switch Off • Ducks Don't Get Wet • Feel the Wind • The Skeleton Inside You • Digging Up Dinosaurs • Tornado Alert • The Sun: Our Nearest Star • The Beginning of the Earth • Eclipse • Dinosaur Bones • Glaciers • Snakes Are Hunters • Danger—Icebergs! • Comets • Evolution • Rockets and Satellites • The Planets in Our Solar System • The Moon Seems to Change • Ant Cities • Get Ready for Robots! • Gravity Is a Mystery • Snow Is Falling • Journey into a Black Hole • What Makes Day and Night • Air Is All Around You • Turtle Talk • What the Moon Is Like • Hurricane Watch • Sunshine Makes the Seasons • My Visit to the Dinosaurs • The BASIC Book • Bits and Bytes • Germs Make Me Sick! • Flash, Crash, Rumble, and Roll • Volcanoes • Dinosaurs Are Different • What Happens to a Hamburger • Meet the Computer • How to Talk to Your Computer • Rock Collecting • Is There Life in Outer Space? • All Kinds of Feet • Flying Giants of Long Ago • Rain and Hail • Why I Cough, Sneeze, Shiver, Hiccup & Yawn • You Can't Make a Move Without Your Muscles • The Sky Is Full of Stars • No Measles, No Mumps for Me

The *Let's-Read-and-Find-Out Science Book* series was originated by Dr. Franklyn M. Branley, Astronomer Emeritus and former Chairman of the American Museum-Hayden Planetarium, and was formerly co-edited by him and Dr. Roma Gans, Professor Emeritus of Childhood Education, Teachers College, Columbia University. For a complete catalog of Let's-Read-and-Find-Out Science Books, write to Thomas Y. Crowell Junior Books, Harper & Row, Publishers, Inc., 10 East 53rd Street, New York, NY 10022.

Shooting Stars
Text copyright © 1989 by Franklyn M. Branley
Illustrations copyright © 1989 by Holly Keller
Typography by Pat Tobin
10 9 8 7 6 5 4 3 2 1
First Edition

Library of Congress Cataloging-in-Publication Data
Branley, Franklyn Mansfield, 1915-
   Shooting stars / by Franklyn M. Branley ; illustrated by Holly Keller. — 1st ed.
      p.   cm. — (Let's-read-and-find-out science book)
   Summary: Explains what shooting stars are, what they are made of, and what happens when they land on Earth.
   ISBN 0-690-04701-0 : $
   ISBN 0-690-04703-7 (lib. bdg.) : $
   1. Meteors—Juvenile literature. 2. Meteoroids—Juvenile literature. 3. Meteorites—Juvenile literature. [1. Meteors. 2. Meteoroids. 3. Meteorites.] I. Keller, Holly, ill. II. Title. III. Series.
QB741.5.B73 1989
523.5'1—dc19
88-14190
CIP
AC

Photo page 23 by D. J. Roddy, U.S. Department of the Interior, Geological Survey; photo page 25 courtesy of NASA.

Shooting Stars

At night when the sky is clear, look for shooting stars. You can see them as soon as the sky is dark. At first you might not see any. You have to keep looking.

Lie down and gaze at the sky for an hour or so. You're almost sure to see at least one an hour. Maybe you'll see more than one. One time I saw so many, it was hard to count them.

A shooting star is not a star. Long ago people called many things in the night sky some kind of star. When they saw a planet, they called it a wandering star. They called comets long-haired stars. When they saw a streak of light, they thought a star was falling out of the sky. They called it a falling star, or a shooting star. Scientists call them meteors. The word comes from a Greek word meaning "something in the air."

9

If you could catch a falling star, you would discover that it is a small bit of ash, or solid material like rock or metal. It might be no larger than a grain of sand. It is called a meteoroid. When a meteoroid makes a light streak in the sky, it is called a meteor.

A meteoroid gets very hot. That's because it rubs against the air as it travels toward Earth. It gets hot, just as your hands do when you rub them together.

The meteoroid gets hot enough to produce light. That's the light you see when you see a shooting star.

Many of the meteoroids that fall toward Earth are so small that they don't make a light streak. Or they may fall during the day, when the sky is so bright that we can't see the light streak. Some scientists think that 100 tons of them fall on Earth every day. Most of them fall into the oceans. When you're outside, some of them may fall on you. But you don't feel them, because many are little more than floating specks of dust.

When a meteoroid strikes Earth, the moon, or another planet, it is called a meteorite. Most meteorites are very small. A few are as large as a marble, or even a baseball. Some are very large. One of the largest ever found is in New York City at the American Museum of Natural History. You can see it there. It was found in Greenland, where the Eskimos called it *Ahnighito*—the tent. It is mostly iron, and it weighs more than 34 tons. The Eskimos made iron knives from pieces of this meteorite.

1982

Sometimes meteorites hit houses. In 1982 one that weighed six pounds crashed through the roof of a house in Wethersfield, Connecticut. It was traveling over 1,000 miles an hour. That was fast enough for it to go right through the ceiling and roll under the dining-room table. Eleven years earlier, in 1971, another meteorite went through the roof of a different house in the same town. That one weighed a little less than a pound.

No one was hit by either of those meteorites. But in 1954 Mrs. Hewlett Hodges, who lived in Sylacauga, Alabama, was hit in the thigh by a meteorite that came right through her ceiling. That one weighed about ten pounds. Her thigh was black and blue for quite a while.

Don't worry about being hit by a meteorite. Mrs. Hodges was the first and only person in the United States ever hit by one. In the last 500 years, only a dozen people in the whole world have been hit.

1954

Many meteorites have fallen on buildings. And many have dug deep holes, or craters, in the Earth. This crater is near Winslow, Arizona. It is 4,150 feet wide and 600 feet deep. You can walk around it and climb down to the bottom.

Meteorites have also fallen on the moon. In the picture, you can see that the moon is covered with craters. Many of them were made when large meteorites crashed into the moon long ago.

Mercury and Mars also have lots of craters. Many of them were dug by meteorites.

Meteorites are visitors from outer space. Billions of dust particles, stones, and rocks are in orbit around the sun. Some of them have been there since Earth began. Many of the bits of ash and dust were left behind by comets as they traveled through space. When Earth moves through clouds of these particles, they make shooting stars—sometimes so many that they fill the sky.

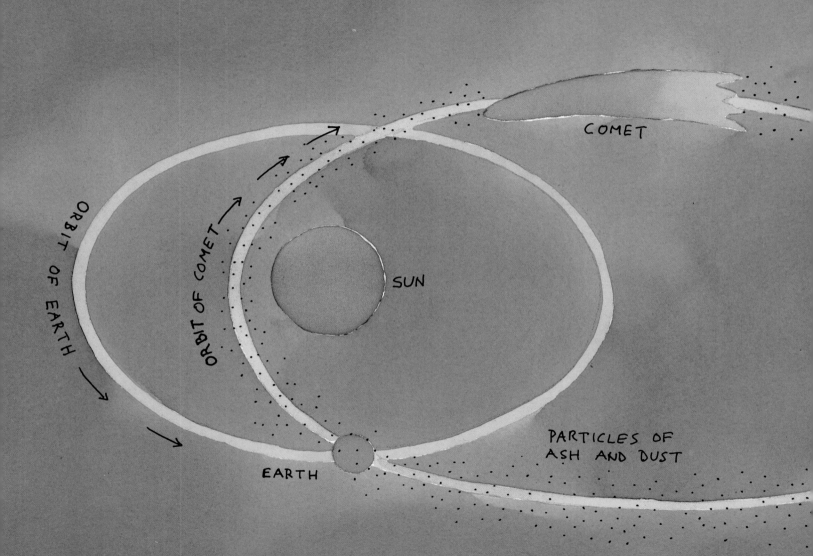

Keep watching for shooting stars. They seem to be far away, but most of them are less than 60 miles above the Earth. One night you may see one that seems a lot closer. You may be able to trace where it lands. You might even find the meteorite.

That's what happened in Mexico. In 1969 people saw a sky full of shooting stars. Later, almost two tons of meteorites were found by people who saw them land.

1969

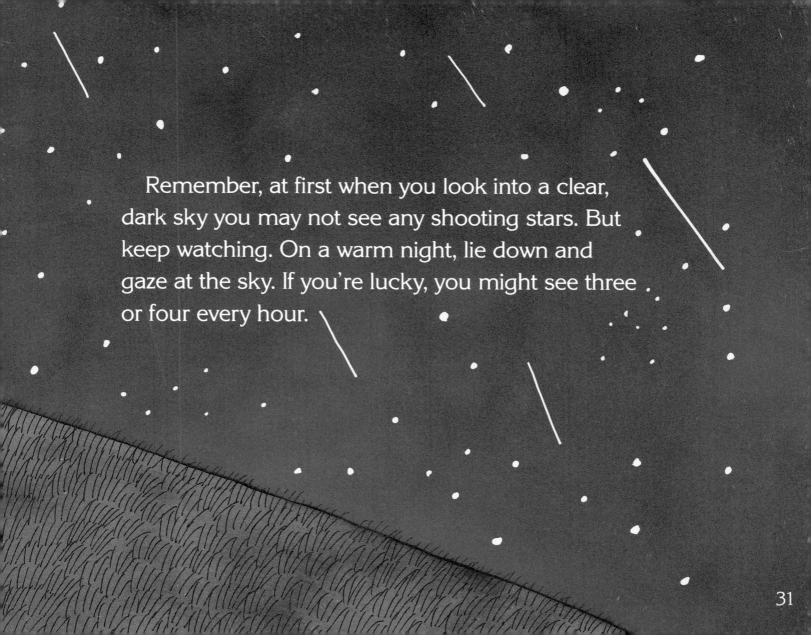

Remember, at first when you look into a clear, dark sky you may not see any shooting stars. But keep watching. On a warm night, lie down and gaze at the sky. If you're lucky, you might see three or four every hour.

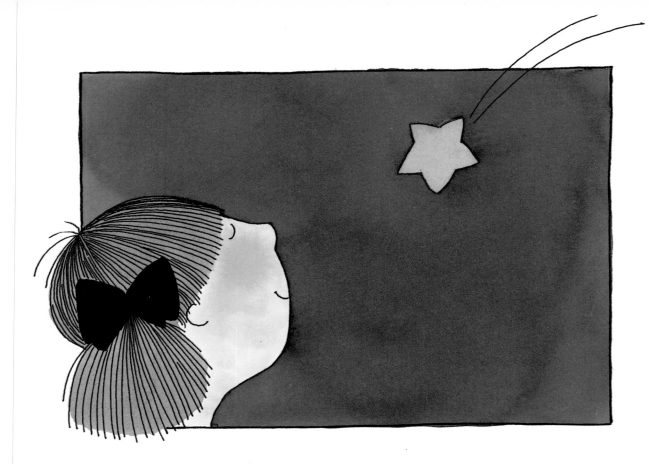

When you see one, make a wish. Some people
say that wishes come true when they are made on
a shooting star. Who knows—maybe they are right.